Walking the Black Cat

OTHER BOOKS BY CHARLES SIMIC

A Wedding in Hell

Hotel Insomnia

The Book of Gods and Devils

Unending Blues

Weather Forecast for Utopia and Vicinity

Selected Poems

Austerities

Classic Ballroom Dances

Charon's Cosmology

Return to a Place Lit by a Glass of Milk

Dismantling the Silence

Walking the Black Cat

POEMS

Charles Simic

HARCOURT BRACE & COMPANY
New York   San Diego   London

Requests for permission to make copies of any part of the work
should be mailed to: Permissions Department, Harcourt Brace & Company,
6277 Sea Harbor Drive, Orlando, Florida 32887-6777.

Library of Congress Cataloging-in-Publication Data
Simic, Charles, 1938–
Walking the black cat : poems/Charles Simic.
p.   cm.
"A Harvest original."
ISBN 0-15-100219-3 (hardcover).—ISBN 0-15-600481-X (pbk.)
I. Title.
PS3569.I4725W35   1996
811'.54—dc20   96-17064

The text was set in Centaur.
Designed by Lori McThomas Buley
Printed in the United States of America
First edition
A B C D E

Some of these poems previously appeared in the following magazines, to whose editors grateful acknowledgment is made: *The New Yorker, The Times Literary Supplement, The London Review of Books, Partisan Review, New American Writing, Ploughshares, Boulevard, Harvard Review, Prose Poetry, The Paris Review, Antaeus, Grand Street, Mudfish, Indiana Review, Poetry Ireland Review, Beloit Poetry Journal, The Baffler, The Virginia Quarterly Review, Chicago Review, The Yale Review, Verse, San Diego Reader, The Field, The American Poetry Review, Elle, Double Take, Boston Review* and *Portsmouth Review.*

for Helen

Contents

Dark Corner   1

Mirrors at 4 A.M.   2

Relaxing in a Madhouse   3

Roach Motel   4

Emily's Theme   5

Cameo Appearance   6

The Friends of Heraclitus   7

An Address with Exclamation Points   9

Le Dame e i Cavalieri   10

Shadow Publishing Company   11

Talking to Little Birdies   13

The Master of Ceremonies   14

My Magician   15

Night in the House of Cards   17

On the Road to Somewhere Else   18

What the Gypsies Told my Grandmother while   21
    She Was Still a Young Girl

Little Unwritten Book   22

Winter Evening   23

Have You Met Miss Jones?   24

On the Sagging Porch   26

Dogs Hear It   27

Meditation in the Gutter   28

Charm School   29

Ghosts   30

Under New Management   32
The Conquering Hero Is Tired   33
The Story of Happiness   34
Theatrical Costumes   35
Bed Music   36
Marked Playing Cards   37
The Road in the Clouds   38
Café Paradiso   39
Blindman's Bluff   40
Turn On the Lights   41
At the Cookout   42
Don't Wake the Cards   44
Free the Goldfish   45
Pastoral Harpsichord   46
Kitchen Helper   47
Entertaining the Canary   48
The Forest Walk   49
Slaughterhouse Flies   50
My Darling Premonition   51
Blood Orange   52
October Light   53
First Day of Summer   54
The Preacher Says   55
Sunset's Coloring Book   58
In a Forest of Whispers   59
Lone Tree   60
Make Yourself Invisible   61
Toad's Poolhall   62
Pain   63
Late Train   65
Club Midnight   66

Late Call   67
Official Inquiry among the Grains of Sand   68
The Street Ventriloquist   69
The Father of Lies   70
Against Winter   71
Squinting Suspiciously   72
The Something   73
Collector's Tweezers   74
The Great Picnic   75
Hot Night   76
My Progress on Stilts   77
The Emperor   79
The Anniversary   83

DARK CORNER

Say, how'd you find me?
Ordinarily, I act deaf and dumb, but with you
It's different. Darting in and out
Of doorways, prowling after me
Like a black cat.

Just look at the suckers, I kept
Shouting at the world. It was no use.
They just stepped over me holding on to their hats,
Or lifting their skirts a little
On the way to hell.

He must be crazy, sprawled there
On the sidewalk, his fly unzipped,
His eyes closing. Only you came back
To see how I'm doing,
Only you peeked into every dark corner.

I'm a bird fluttering in flight.
Find me a nice, large cage with the door open.
Back me out of here with your kisses.
My shoes need laces.
My pants need your finger to hold them up.

MIRRORS AT 4 A.M.

You must come to them sideways
In rooms webbed in shadow,
Sneak a view of their emptiness
Without them catching
A glimpse of you in return.

The secret is,
Even the empty bed is a burden to them,
A pretense.
They are more themselves keeping
The company of a blank wall,
The company of time and eternity

Which, begging your pardon,
Cast no image
As they admire themselves in the mirror,
While you stand to the side
Pulling a hanky out
To wipe your brow surreptitiously.

They had already attached the evening's tears to the windowpanes.

The general was busy with the ant farm in his head.

The holy saints in their tombs were burning, all except one who was a prisoner of a dark-haired movie star.

Moses wore a false beard and so did Lincoln.

X reproduced the Socratic method of interrogation by demonstrating the ceiling's ignorance.

"They stole the secret of the musical matchbook from me," confided Adam.

"The world's biggest rooster was going to make me famous," said Eve.

O to run naked over the darkening meadow after the cold shower!

In the white pavilion the nurse was turning water into wine.

Hurry home, dark cloud.

ROACH MOTEL

The fears of my mother,
And I their projectionist
Cranking the projector.

An evening of noir films.
The electric chair is in it,
And so are the cops.
I'm smoking a cheap cigar,
Playing poker with a scar-faced killer
And a fat woman with a husky voice.
She drinks gin out of a bottle,
Sways her hips to the radio,
Has wedding plans.
At daybreak, a web of twisting shadows
Cast by a ceiling fan.
I have holes in my socks,
An asthmatic wheeze
When I kneel down to pray.

I also have a long tail
And look like a monkey
Because I keep lying all the time.

EMILY'S THEME

My dear trees, I no longer recognize you
In that wintry light.
You brought me a reminder I can do without:
The world is old, it was always old,
There's nothing new in it this afternoon.
The garden could've been a padlocked window
Of a pawnshop I was studying
With every item in it dust-covered.

Each one of my thoughts was being ghostwritten
By anonymous authors. Each time they hit
A cobwebbed typewriter key, I shudder.
Luckily, dark came quickly today.
Soon the neighbors were burning leaves,
And perhaps a few other things too.
Later, I saw the children run around the fire,
Their faces demonic in its flames.

CAMEO APPEARANCE

I had a small, nonspeaking part
In a bloody epic. I was one of the
Bombed and fleeing humanity.
In the distance our great leader
Crowed like a rooster from a balcony,
Or was it a great actor
Impersonating our great leader?

That's me there, I said to the kiddies.
I'm squeezed between the man
With two bandaged hands raised
And the old woman with her mouth open
As if she were showing us a tooth

That hurts badly. The hundred times
I rewound the tape, not once
Could they catch sight of me
In that huge gray crowd,
That was like any other gray crowd.

Trot off to bed, I said finally.
I know I was there. One take
Is all they had time for.
We ran, and the planes grazed our hair,
And then they were no more
As we stood dazed in the burning city,
But, of course, they didn't film that.

THE FRIENDS OF HERACLITUS

Your friend has died, with whom
You roamed the streets,
At all hours, talking philosophy.
So, today you went alone,
Stopping often to change places
With your imaginary companion,
And argue back against yourself
On the subject of appearances:
The world we see in our heads
And the world we see daily,
So difficult to tell apart
When grief and sorrow bow us over.

You two often got so carried away
You found yourselves in strange neighborhoods
Lost among unfriendly folk,
Having to ask for directions
While on the verge of a supreme insight,
Repeating your question
To an old woman or a child
Both of whom may have been deaf and dumb.

What was that fragment of Heraclitus
You were trying to remember
As you stepped on the butcher's cat?
Meantime, you yourself were lost
Between someone's new black shoe
Left on the sidewalk

And the sudden terror and exhilaration
At the sight of a girl
Dressed up for a night of dancing
Speeding by on roller skates.

AN ADDRESS WITH EXCLAMATION POINTS

I accused History of gluttony;
Happiness of anorexia!

O History, cruel and mystical,
You ate Russia as if it were
A pot of white beans cooked with
Sausage, smoked ribs and ham hocks!

O Happiness, whose every miserly second
Is brimming with eternity!
You sat over a dish of vanilla custard
Without ever touching it!

The silent heavens were peeved!
They made the fair skies at sunset
Flash their teeth and burp from time to time,
Till our wedding picture slid off the wall.

The kitchen is closed, the waiters shouted!
No more vineyard snails in garlic butter!
No more ox tripe fried in onions!
We have only tears of happiness left!

LE DAME E I CAVALIERI

Considering our resources, it was a staggering sum.
A dozen birds of paradise spit-roasted with
Red and yellow cherries wedged in their beaks.
Here was finally something to make amends
For all the greasy burgers and fries we lived on.
It was like a church choir barging into a whorehouse;
I mean, our anticipation and sinful joy
At the prospect of such a feast. Fake Madonna
Biting your nails, and you, too, Doc,
Shaking hands all around, get over here!
Our quarters are cramped, but we can all fit
If we sit in each other's laps. It'll be
Like a séance and we the twelve psychic crime solvers.
Mr. Undertaker, and you Mr. Corpse,
Let me be the first to say, this bird of heaven
Looks good but tastes something awful.

SHADOW PUBLISHING COMPANY

This couple strolling arm in arm
Must be figments of someone's revery.
They stop often to linger over a kiss,
But when people look their way,
It's as if they do not see them.

It's the heat, the blue dusk,
The air of enchantment
On the street of overgrown lilacs
And screened porches
Where a door is already open for them.

An old woman waits in the dim entrance
With a pitcher of cold lemonade
And two tall glasses on a tray.
She wants them to rest awhile
In her own wedding bed and they obey.

Her late husband was an eye doctor.
His surgical instruments lie in a glass case
Gleaming like cold moonlight.
In dark cuffs, he made the blind see
By removing their bandages.

In a room shaded against the heat,
With a few slender lines of light
Converging on the high ceiling,
And that strange sense of taking on the life
Of someone unknown just then,

Lying there, closing one's eyes in revery,
A figment among figments
Living one of their blessed moments
Without recognizing the century,
Only the scent of the lilacs on the pillow.

TALKING TO LITTLE BIRDIES

Not a peep out of you now
After all the racket early this morning.
Are you begging pardon of me
Hidden up there among the leaves,
Or are your brains momentarily overtaxed?

You savvy a few things I don't:
The overlooked sunflower seed worth a holler;
The traffic of cats in the yard;
Strangers leaving the widow's house,
Tieless and wearing crooked grins.

Or have you got wind of the world's news?
Some new horror I haven't heard about yet?
Which one of you is so bold as to warn me
Our sweet setup is in danger?

Kids are playing soldiers down the road,
Pointing their rifles and playing dead.
Little birdies, are you sneaking wary looks
In the thick foliage
As you watch me go to speak to them?

THE MASTER OF CEREMONIES

He's shouting again from the rooftop
And pointing,
Pointing and bowing down from the waist
As he introduces the evening performance:

The baby in the crib is playing with his father's
Black sock, pulling it over its head.
In another window,
A woman with a stem of a red rose between her teeth
Has got hold of a tiger cat by its tail
And for some reason won't let it go.

And now for a bit of snow.

All those normally incapable of happiness
Are catching flakes on their eyelids,
On their tongues
As they run amuck in the street.

Pastry chef, I believe, you're next.

MY MAGICIAN

Someone pulled me out of a tux sleeve,
Doctor, hanging for my dear life
At the end of a long white scarf.
I fluttered over my magician.
I flew around the hushed theater.

Saturdays, at nine and at midnight,
He sawed me in half,
While I lay in the coffin
Next to my naked bride.
I never got to see his face
Even when the applause started.

We held our breaths under his hat.
Two look-alike dummies, we took
Turns sitting on his knee.
Through a row of wooden teeth
We spoke of God the Father.
Then we vanished in a pack of cards.

We were terrified and happy.
One instant he was swallowing fire,
The next he was spitting it
With the two of us riding the long flame
Like a coach into the sunset.

Between his tricks I was nowhere
I could think of:
Not in this world with its chained bear
And its magic mirror,
Not in that other
Where the white clouds float and sheep graze.

NIGHT IN THE HOUSE OF CARDS

A lot of dust has settled today,
The Evening News said.
The walls still shook from time to time
As if the night was a truck
Loaded with gravel rumbling by.

Then it was quiet.
The builder of the house of cards
Had rushed off
Holding her masked children by the hand.
I didn't dare light another match
And look at the walls.
There were pictures everywhere of bearded men
And their bearded wives.
The match flame made them dance
So that afterwards
I lay sleepless in the dark.

In the night, the wind
That chills the stars to a squint
Blew a card off the roof
Up one of its dark sleeves.
The dawn sky was like a torn red dress
The girl on the back of the card wore.

ON THE ROAD TO SOMEWHERE ELSE

The leaves made us think
Of a letter trembling in someone's hand.
In fact, many letters in many hands,
And then they no longer did.

There was a bedraggled old woman
Walking
With two gray boards on her back
Joined into a cross
To cook her dinner with,

And then,
We were somewhere else.

The painter of doll faces
Dipped a small brush into a red jar,
In a cramped shed
With its door open
And a hen or two looking in,
Their heads bobbing in approval
At the way he raises his eyebrows,
Purses his lips
And makes the doll's cheeks blush.

*

At the end of a dark dead-end street
Not far from the railroad tracks
Where the night train's brightly lit
Coaches clatter by one by one,
And then their noise recedes,
Thins out to a ghost of itself,
So that now the leaves' lazy shiver
Can be heard, and the sniffles
Of the girl who's been crying,
But is now ready to walk home
Closely shadowed by her beau.
His face like a carved pumpkin head
In the quick flare of a match.

WHAT THE GYPSIES TOLD MY GRANDMOTHER WHILE SHE WAS STILL A YOUNG GIRL

War, illness and famine will make you their favorite
    grandchild.
You'll be like a blind person watching a silent movie.
You'll chop onions and pieces of your heart
    into the same hot skillet.
Your children will sleep in a suitcase tied with a rope.
Your husband will kiss your breasts every night
    as if they were two gravestones.

Already the crows are grooming themselves
    for you and your people.
Your oldest son will lie with flies on his lips
    without smiling or lifting his hand.
You'll envy every ant you meet in your life
    and every roadside weed.
Your body and soul will sit on separate stoops
    chewing the same piece of gum.

Little cutie, are you for sale? the devil will say.
The undertaker will buy a toy for your grandson.
Your mind will be a hornet's nest even on your
    deathbed.
You will pray to God but God will hang a sign
    that He's not to be disturbed.
Question no further, that's all I know.

LITTLE UNWRITTEN BOOK

Rocky was a regular guy, a loyal friend.
The trouble was he was only a cat.
Let's practice, he'd say, and he'd pounce
On his shadow on the wall.
I have to admit, I didn't learn a thing.
I often sat watching him sleep.
If the birds tried to have a bit of fun in the yard,
He opened one eye.
I even commended him for good behavior.

He was black except for the white gloves he wore.
He played the piano in the parlor
By walking over its keys back and forth.
With exquisite tact he chewed my ear
If I wouldn't get up from my chair.
Then one day he vanished. I called.
I poked in the bushes.
I walked far into the woods.

The mornings were the hardest. I'd put out
A saucer of milk at the back door.
Peekaboo, a bird called out. She knew.
At one time we had ten farmhands working for us.
I'd make a megaphone with my hands and call.
I still do, though it's been years.
Rocky, I cry!
And now the bird is silent too.

WINTER EVENING

These hunches I get, cold shivers
At the way the light
Makes bloodstains on the house wall,
I'm scared to trust a sparrow,
I won't come near the cat.

Destiny marks you early in the day
With a knowing finger,
Then busies itself setting up the props,
Painting the scenery.

My love's window was on fire
With the sunset.
Her hair was red.
The pillow she carried in her arms
Was like a baby.

Quiet as a bread crumb,
I stood and watched.
All around me birds had fallen silent.
And then the clouds moved
Their tragic robes,
And so did the night.

HAVE YOU MET MISS JONES?

I have. At the funeral
Pulling down her skirt to cover her knees
While inadvertently
Showing us her cleavage
Down to the tip of her nipples.

A complete stranger, wobbly on her heels,
Negotiating the exit
With the assembled mourners
Eyeing her rear end
With visible interest.

Presidential hopefuls
Will continue to lie to the people
As we sit here bowed.
New hatreds will sweep the globe
Faster than the weather.
Sewer rats will sniff around
Lit cash machines
While we sigh over the departed.

And her beauty will live on, no matter
What any one of these black-clad,
Grim veterans of every wake,
Every prison gate and crucifixion,
Sputters about her discourtesy.

Miss Jones, you'll be safe
With the insomniacs. You'll triumph
Where they pour wine from a bottle
Wrapped in a white napkin,

Eat sausage with pan-fried potatoes,
And grow misty-eyed remembering

The way you walked past the open coffin,
Past the stiff with his nose in the air
Taking his long siesta.
A cute little number an old man said,
But who was she?
Miss Jones, the guest book proclaimed.

ON THE SAGGING PORCH

Sits the grim-looking president
Of the local SPCA
As you come walking on all fours,
Making it plain you are lost,
Have a bad limp,
Need a brand-new master today.

He can use a stick if he wants to.
You desire an insignificant,
Silent and mostly sedentary life,
With your travels reduced
To one or two dark corners
And an occasional visit to the kitchen.

He makes no sign to acknowledge you.
His eyes are far away.
Is he blind, is he crazy?
You keep asking yourself.
His dog, coming over to sniff
And growl at you a little,
Is called Judas.

DOGS HEAR IT

This machinery is very ancient.
It lumbers towards me
With all its rusty parts throbbing.
A great big contraption made of air,
Made of phantasms.
Its wheels sulk. Dust chokes them,
Nasty bits of gravel
Full of their own spunk.

Some nights it's so loud,
I sit up in bed.
Hamlet's ghost walking the hallways
Of a motel in Vegas—

He draweth likeness after likeness
Of what's hidden in plain sight—
Who? Who? I shouted, startled,
Until the bride and groom next door
Told me to rest my jaws.

MEDITATION IN THE GUTTER

Of things undescribable!
Things unspeakable!
The scent of summer night.
Rabbit paté made with Vouvray wine
The flutes in the Andes.
Dark treetops against moonlit sky.
The street at dusk
Like a fading memory of a golden moment
At the vanishing point.

I sat leaning against a mailbox
Where years earlier I dropped a love letter.
It was still there whispering to me,
And then it wasn't.
A silent, sunlit corner, empty
But for a black cat about to cross,
One of its paws raised
As if trying to feel the cunning threads
By which its life, too, is being held.

CHARM SCHOOL

Madame Gabrielle, were you really French?
And what were those heavy books
You made them balance on top of their heads,
Young women with secret aspirations,
We saw strolling past the row of windows
In the large room above Guido's barbershop?

On the same floor was the office of an obscure
Weekly preaching bloody revolution.
Men with raised collars and roving eyes
Wandered in and out. When they conspired
They spat and pulled down the yellow shades,
Not to raise them or open the windows again

Until the summer heat came and your students
Wore dresses with their shoulders bared
As they promenaded with books on their heads,
And the bald customer in the barbershop
Sat sweating while overseeing in the mirror
His three remaining hairs being combed.

GHOSTS

It's Mr. Brown looking much better
Than he did in the morgue.
He's brought me a huge carp
In a bloodstained newspaper.
What an odd visit.
I haven't thought of him in years.

Linda is with him and so is Sue.
Two pale and elegant fading memories
Holding each other by the hand.
Even their lipstick is fresh
Despite all the scientific proofs
To the contrary.

Is Linda going to cook the fish?
She turns and gazes in the direction
Of the kitchen while Sue
Continues to watch me mournfully.
I don't believe any of it,
And still I'm scared stiff.

I know of no way to respond,
So I do nothing.
The windows are open. The air's thick
With the scent of magnolias.
Drops of evening rain are dripping
From the dark and heavy leaves.
I take a deep breath; I close my eyes.

Dear specters, I don't even believe
You are here, so how is it
You're making me comprehend
Things I would rather not know just yet?

It's the way you stare past me
At what must already be my own ghost,
Before taking your leave,
As unexpectedly as you came in,
Without one of us breaking the silence.

UNDER NEW MANAGEMENT

The tunnel of love at the fair.
The oompah band.
The long-legged drum majorette.
The pebble in my shoe.
Little birds sitting on the telephone wire.
Hotel of the Great Secret.
The out-of-tune piano.
Death, the butterfingered waiter.
The American lynch mob.
The Gypsy who slips me advice.
Moonlit and deserted parking lots.

THE CONQUERING HERO IS TIRED

Often I sit at your window
For hours on end watching you snooze.
You could be in medical school
Sawing a cadaver.
You could be leading men into battle,
Donning judicial robes,
Inventing a new potato peeler, and so forth.
My kind admonitions, my well-meant
Remonstrances you receive
By turning your face to the wall.

Blue dusk and the night's gloom
Are your true cronies.
Streets time forgot where fire-sale leaflets
Fly about, the ten-year-old assassin
Twirls his gun, the cats shield themselves
Under rusted cars.

For Christ's sake, turn off the light! you plead.
I'm afraid it can't be done.
The bright sunlight, the blue sky,
The little birds hopping and chirping on the sill
Are all perfectly legal.

THE STORY OF HAPPINESS

Happiness, unknown woman,
There's a childhood picture
Of the two of us,
Your hands are covering my eyes,
All but your arms are cut off.

I always hoped you'll return.
I'll be doing nothing in particular,
Barely keeping an eye on the person
Ahead of me at the checkout counter,
When that delicious blindness
Will again sweep me off my feet.

It's a baffle, I said only yesterday.
Then I raised my beer glass
And invited everyone present
To drink to my future happiness,
When the bartender asked me
To please stop making a disturbance.

My happiness is busy making others happy,
I continued under my breath.
It will come to me yet:
I'll be tinkling the little iron bell
On a desk of an antique store...
I'll be on a motorcycle flying at dusk
Over the Nevada desert, when...

THEATRICAL COSTUMES

A present from neighborly burglars
For us to dress up
On a dull day
In a manner fantastic

Cutting a great dash
As we descend the stairs
In our powdered wigs and high-heeled shoes
Into the busy street,
Crossing it against the screeching
Traffic, and entering
The Burger Heaven with a swish
Of your long skirts
And not even a Say what?
From the astonished customers

You are dressed like Marie Antoinette
And I am all in black
Like her executioner
Or her father confessor.
It's New York City. It's hot.
The fire alarms are ringing everywhere.

The French Queen is putting
A lot of ketchup on her fries.
Her executioner is inserting
A lit ciggie in each ear
And blowing the smoke out his mouth.

BED MUSIC

Our love was new,
But your bedsprings were old.
In the flat below,
They stopped eating
With forks in the air.

They made the old sourpuss
Climb the stairs
And squint through the keyhole,
While we went right ahead
Making the springs toot,

Playing "Low Down on the Bayou,"
Playing "Big Leg Mama,"
Playing "Shake It Baby"
And "Carolina Shout."

That was the limit!
They called the fire brigade.
They called the Law.
They could've brought some hooch,
We told the cops.

MARKED PLAYING CARDS

I took my TV and bass fiddle to the pawnshop.
Then I had my car stolen and everything in it.
This morning I'm down to a windbreaker and house
    slippers,
But I feel cheerful, even though it's snowing.
This proves she loves me, I said to the crowd
Waiting for the bus. They were afraid to look my way.

I let myself be reduced to rags, I explained.
I marked playing cards to cheat against myself.
All my life I kept raising the stakes, knowing
That each new loss assured me of her complete love.
(The bus was late, so they had to hear the rest.)
I told them that I never met her, but that I was certain
She has a premonition of my existence,
As I do of hers. Perhaps this is the moment
She comes along and recognizes me standing here?

Because my mind was busy with our first kiss,
I didn't hear the bus arrive and leave.
High over the roofs, the sky was already clearing.
I still had the greasy cards in my pocket.
With my bad luck, I surmised, she was due by nightfall.
Shuffling through the snow and shivering,
I was ready to bet the rest of my clothes on her.

THE ROAD IN THE CLOUDS

Your undergarments and mine,
Sent flying around the room
Like a storm of white feathers
Striking the window and ceiling.

Something like repressed laughter
Is in the air
As we lie in sweet content
Drifting off to sleep
With the treetops in purple light

And the sudden memory
Of riding a bicycle
Using no hands
Down a steep winding road
To the blue sea.

CAFÉ PARADISO

My chicken soup thickened with pounded young almonds
My blend of winter greens.
Dearest tagliatelle with mushrooms, fennel, anchovies,
Tomatoes and vermouth sauce.
Beloved monkfish braised with onions, capers
And green olives.
Give me your tongue tasting of white beans and garlic,
Sexy little assortment of formaggi and frutta!
I want to drown with you in red wine like a pear,
Then sleep in a macédoine of wild berries with cream.

BLINDMAN'S BLUFF

Death's an early riser.
You've got to be real quick
To slip under his arm
Stretched toward you in the street.

His nails brushing you,
Press yourself against the wall,
Eyes wide open,
While he spins around,

In his white blindfold,
Arms like a Dutch windmill,
Or like huge scissors
On the pavement already crowded
With schoolchildren.

TURN ON THE LIGHTS

A tiny, no-see fly,
Buzzing, pestering us
All night long.
Its tiny hell
Pressing the sides
Of its tiny head.

Here, take the scissors
In your hand,
These bird-shaped ones.
Squeeze them quickly,
Or ever so slowly.
Your nails, I notice,
Are red already
And bitten raw in the dark.

AT THE COOKOUT

The wives of my friends
Have the air
Of having shared a secret.
Their eyes are lowered
But when we ask them
What for
They only glance at each other
And smile,
Which only increases our desire
To know...

Something they did
Long ago,
Heedless of the consequences,
That left
Such a lingering sweetness?

Is that the explanation
For the way
They rest their chins
In the palms of their hands,
Their eyes closed
In the summer heat?

Come tell us,
Or give us a hint.
Trace a word or just a single letter
In the wine
Spilled on the table.

No reply. Both of them
Lovey-dovey
With the waning sunlight
And the evening breeze
On their faces.

The husbands drinking
And saying nothing,
Dazed and mystified as they are
By their wives' power
To give
And take away happiness,
As if their heads
Were crawling with snakes.

DON'T WAKE THE CARDS

Since my chronic bad luck
Vanished in my love's deck of cards,
I step around them softly,
I won't open the window on windy days.

I unpin her long black hair
And strip down her dress myself,
Lest their flutter stir the dead air
And make the cards fly.

I tell her, Don't even think
About picking up a broom
Or dancing with your boobs flapping.
Lie back in my arms

And watch the light fall
Golden over us
In wordless silence.
Don't wake the damn cards.

FREE THE GOLDFISH

A pet store window
With an aquarium
We pressed our noses against
Every night.

For light, the goldfish had
A single bulb
On a long naked wire
Tied into a noose.

They swam to and fro glancing
Over their shoulders
At the empty shelves,
The street beyond with its dark shadows,

Its rows of parked cars
On which a few large snowflakes
Fell carefully
As if not to make a sound.

PASTORAL HARPSICHORD

A house with a screened-in porch
On the road to nowhere.
The missus topless because of the heat,
A bag of Frito Banditos in her lap.
President Bush on TV
Watching her every bite.

Poor reception, that's the one
Advantage we have here,
I said to the mutt lying at my feet
And sighing in sympathy.
On another channel the preacher
Came chaperoned by his ghost
When he shut his eyes full of tears
To pray for dollars.

"Bring me another beer," I said to her ladyship,
And when she wouldn't oblige,
I went out to make chamber music
Against the sunflowers in the yard.

KITCHEN HELPER

I'm your chopping board,
Your frying pan
And the knife you mince
The onions
And cut your finger with.

In the garden the leaves
Are flying about
Like small game birds.
With raised glasses
Your drunken guests
Are playing at Last Supper,
Holding the table
And hollering,
The sky is falling.

Clever cook, let me
Steal your glasses for a moment
To peek into the pot
Where the cause of their happiness
Is bubbling over
With many secret ingredients
And seasonings
Only you know the names of.

ENTERTAINING THE CANARY

Yellow feathers,
Is it true
You chirp to the cop
On the beat?

Desist. Turn your
Nervous gaze
At the open bathroom door
Where I'm soaping

My love's back
And putting my chin on her shoulder
So I can do the same for her
Breasts and crotch.

Sing. Flutter your wings
As if you were applauding,
Or I'll throw her black slip
Over your gilded cage.

THE FOREST WALK

Today we took a long walk in the forest.
There we met a couple walking
Arm in arm with eyes closed.
The forest is a dream you had
When you were little, they told us.
Then the two of them were gone.

Even in the afternoon the narrow path
Was busy with shadows.
They had many dark secrets among them,
The trees did.
Shhhh is all we kept hearing.
The leaf we plucked and held in our hands
Appeared genuinely frightened.

The night threw open its birdcage.
The trees pretended to protect us.
In a fit of passion they'd rise
Against the slightest sough of wind,
Only to fall back
Into long minutes of listening.

Let's stay here tonight, you said,
And I agreed, but then we didn't.
You had left the key in the car,
And the video store was about to close.
We were running now.
We could see the ice-cream truck.
We could see the plane's landing lights.

SLAUGHTERHOUSE FLIES

Evenings, they ran their bloody feet
Over the pages of my schoolbooks.
With eyes closed, I can still hear
The trees on our street
Saying a moody farewell to summer,

And someone, under our window, recalling
The silly old cows hesitating,
Growing suddenly suspicious
Just as the blade drops down on them.

MY DARLING PREMONITION

She's got something important to tell me,
Though, I suspect,
She doesn't know a damn thing.
She just likes to put on an air of mystery
To impress me. So,

When I think she's paying
A quick visit to the future
On my behalf,
She's right here behind my back
Making faces.

Stop shilly-shallying and lying to me!
I warned her.
And please don't wear black.
You are not getting ready to go to a funeral,
Are you?

I could see she was miffed.
I believe she actually had tears in her eyes,
And was trembling.
But what about?
She wouldn't say.

BLOOD ORANGE

It looks so dark the end of the world may be near.
I believe it's going to rain.
The birds in the park are silent.
Nothing is what it seems to be,
Nor are we.

There's a tree on our street so big
We can all hide in its leaves.
We won't need any clothes either.
I feel as old as a cockroach, you said.
In my head, I'm a passenger on a ghost ship.

Not even a sigh outdoors now.
If a child was left on our doorstep,
It must be asleep.
Everything is teetering on the edge of everything
With a polite smile.

It's because there are things in this world
That just can't be helped, you said.
Right then, I heard the blood orange
Roll off the table and with a thud
Lie cracked open on the floor.

OCTOBER LIGHT

That same light by which I saw her last
Made me close my eyes now in revery,
Remembering how she sat in the garden

With a red shawl over her shoulders
And a small book in her lap,
Once in a long while looking up

With the day's brightness on her face,
As if to appraise something of utmost seriousness
She has just read at least twice,

With the sky clear and open to view,
Because the leaves had already fallen
And lay still around her two feet.

FIRST DAY OF SUMMER

Birds shit while they sing
The white butterfly sips wine left in the glass

And I'm looking for my toy trumpet

THE PREACHER SAYS

Regiments of the damned, halt!

So, we turned to take a better look
At the spread eagle on the sidewalk.

There he was, hair combed over his eyes.

Abominations, he called after us,

Everything crummy and screwed up since Adam
Is thanks to you!

Let's see you turn water into wine!

Let's see you get down on your knees and pray!

*

You are nothing but a lightning bug
The night flicks off its sleeve!

An abandoned movie lot in the desert
With its windows broken.

Every one of your wishes has ridden off
Into the sunset.

Raise your arms in farewell,
Ding-a-ling,

The red wind is looking for you.

Even the rats when they die
Are going to a better world.

Even the scuffed shoes
Of Catholic boys.

Even you with a hearing aid

And a nose on you
Like the key to the firehouse.

Murderers crawling in the playpen,
How big you've grown.

I hear your baby talk,

And the way you rock your wooden horse

The day you're thinking about
Wringing my neck.

In the dims, the murky dusks,
Of your brain on Judgment Day,

It'll be like 100,000 firecrackers
Going off

All at the same time.

✳

The preacher says:

I'd like to be God's video game
In a closed penny arcade

On a dark street,

Its orange lights flashing all by themselves

All night long.

SUNSET'S COLORING BOOK

The blue trees argue with the red wind.

The white mare has a peacock for a servant.

The hawk brings the night in its claws.

The golden mountain doesn't exist.

The golden mountain touches the black sky.

IN A FOREST OF WHISPERS

There is a blind hen
Pecking at a grain of gold
A stream so cold
It's afraid to flow

An escaped convict talking of home
To a withered tree
And death's favorite crow
Sitting in it

In a forest of whispers
Where a lone ant
Just raised on his back
A charred straw

LONE TREE

A tree spooked
By its own evening whispers.
Afraid to rustle,
Just now
Bewitched by the distant sunset

Making a noise full of deep
Misgivings,
Like bloody razor blades
Being shuffled,

And then again the quiet.
The birds too terror-stricken
To make their own comment.
Every leaf to every other leaf
An apparition,
A separate woe.

Bare twig:
A finger of suspicion.

MAKE YOURSELF INVISIBLE

Drew islands with palm trees,
My sister did.
The beaches were empty.
We wanted to lie on their hot sand
And drink lemonade.

Read your book and be quiet,
They yelled at us from the kitchen.

That spring we could smell lilacs
During the blackout.
Boom! Boom! The bombs fell
While a dog barked bravely
In someone's back yard.

Make yourselves invisible,
The old witch said.
From now on, we were breadcrumbs
In a dark forest
Where the little red birds
Had just fallen silent.

TOAD'S POOLHALL

I'm tired of all this, I said,
While shutting one eye
And calculating the odds with the other.
In my mind already I was larger than life,
Fit for the screen
Of a drive-in movie in the desert.

I stood on the empty highway
With my thumb raised.
The sky over me
Was like a western star's dress
Strewn with sequins.

See how far you'll get,
The one we called the Theologian
Muttered behind my back.
He read the writings of Calvin
And savored their meanness.

Oh, but the June sunrise
In the back of a pickup truck!
The radio playing
Old-time fiddle music...
And then I missed the shot.

PAIN

I was doing nothing in particular,
Spring was coming,
When out of the blue
I grabbed my side,
Surprised by this most awful of rewards
From which at first I wanted to
Run away and couldn't.

The pain stayed until I knew its childlike
Cruelty and innocence,
Its pettiness too.
Fear came to keep it company:
A theater director
Wearing a black cape
And offering a series of boring melodramas.

I wanted Reason to defend me.
Instead, it sought causes
Of my depravity,
Smaller reasons like piano keys
I could play to my heart's content,
While the pain continued.

Impervious to argument,
The pain came closer,
Throbbing with impatience
As if to ingratiate itself.
Mean old Fate, I complained,
All you've ever given me
Is the satisfaction of moaning
And keeping my love awake.

"When all of reality hurts
You'll understand."
But it was too early for understanding.
There were just my eyes burning
With fever and curiosity
In the dark windowpane
I sometimes used as a mirror.

LATE TRAIN

A few couples walking off into the dark.
In the very spot they vanished
The trees full of leaves are swaying wildly
Without making the slightest sound.
The train, too, sits still in the station.

I remember a friend telling me once
How he woke up in a long train
Put out of service in a railroad yard.
In the dining car the tables were all set
With wine glasses and fresh flowers.
He could see the moon's lost white glove.

Here, though, there's nothing but night.
In the empty coach, far in the back,
I thought I could see one shadowy passenger
Raising his pale hand to wave to me
Or to put a watch to his ear,
While I stretched my neck to hear the tick.

CLUB MIDNIGHT

Are you the sole owner of a seedy nightclub?

Are you its sole customer, sole bartender,
Sole waiter prowling around the empty tables?

Do you put on wee-hour girlie shows
With dead stars of black-and-white films?

Is your office upstairs over the neon lights,
Or down deep in the dank rat cellar?

Are bearded Russian thinkers your silent partners?
Do you have a doorman by the name of Dostoyevsky?

Is Fu Manchu coming tonight?
Is Miss Emily Dickinson?

Do you happen to have an immortal soul?
Do you have a sneaky suspicion that you have none?

Is that why you throw a white pair of dice,
In the dark, long after the joint closes?

LATE CALL

A message for you,
Mouse turd:

You double-crossed us.
You were supposed to get yourself
Crucified
For the sake of Truth...

Who, me?

A mere crumb, thankfully,
Overlooked on a dinner table,
Lacking in enthusiasm...
An average nobody.

Oh, the worries...

In the dark windowpane
My mouth gutted open.
Aghast.
The panel of judges all black-hooded.

It must be a joke.
A misunderstanding, fellows.
A wrong number, surely?
A slipup?
An erratum?

OFFICIAL INQUIRY AMONG THE GRAINS OF SAND

You're wholly anonymous.
You believe yourself living incognito
In the rear of a weed-choked,
Rat-infested,
Long-vacant seaside villa.
A gray gull,
Most likely the chief snoop
Of a previously unknown
Secret government agency,
Is tiptoeing around importantly.

Aha! At the intersection of
The Visible-Invisible,
Past the lost dog hair,
Past the solitary sugar crumb:
There! With your pants down.
Clutching your mouth in horror.
Without a shadow of a doubt
The indistinguishable you.

THE STREET VENTRILOQUIST

The bearded old man on the corner,
The one drinking out of a brown paper bag,
The one who declares himself
The world's greatest ventriloquist,
We are all his puppets, he says
When he chooses to say anything.

Neon at sundown, lovers carrying tall cages
With frightened songbirds,
Early shadows going to meet
The one and true darkness,
A few sun-struck windows at the horizon,
The blind doomsayer lifting his board
For all to read.

So, I'm the cat's-paw, I said,
And went off shadowboxing
With my own reflection
Appearing and disappearing
In a row of store windows
That already had that seen-a-ghost look.

THE FATHER OF LIES

I have a garden with nothing
But barbed wire and cinder blocks.
My bees go around on crutches.

When they buzz,
It's a lazy afternoon
In the meadow,
When they go gathering
With their hats,
The sky is cloudless,
Birds sing.

The honey in the black glove
Is golden.
Give it to a child
To lick,
Give it to his dying mother
Lying in the shade
Of the old
Sleepwalking tree.

Time is slow. My bees
Are busy
And their eyes are closed.

AGAINST WINTER

The truth is dark under your eyelids.
What are you going to do about it?
The birds are silent; there's no one to ask.
All day long you'll squint at the gray sky.
When the wind blows you'll shiver like straw.

A meek little lamb, you grew your wool
Till they came after you with huge shears.
Flies hovered over your open mouth,
Then they, too, flew off like the leaves,
The bare branches reached after them in vain.

Winter coming. Like the last heroic soldier
Of a defeated army, you'll stay at your post,
Head bared to the first snowflake.
Till a neighbor comes to yell at you,
You're crazier than the weather, Charlie.

SQUINTING SUSPICIOUSLY

I was watching time crawl roachlike,
Shuddering and stopping
As if some of its legs
Had already been plucked.

It still had the whole of infinity
To climb like a kitchen wall.
The very thought of it,
In all likelihood,
Causing these jitters,
These eentsy-weentsy doubts.

It must be the chill, I told myself.
Neither one of us can get warm
Even on a hot night like this.
O cruel Time, you need someone to throw
A blanket over you, and so do I.

THE SOMETHING

Here come my night thoughts
On crutches,
Returning from studying the heavens.
What they thought about
Stayed the same,
Stayed immense and incomprehensible.

My mother and father smile at each other
Knowingly above the mantel.
The cat sleeps on, the dog
Growls in his sleep.
The stove is cold and so is the bed.

Now there are only these crutches
To contend with.
Go ahead and laugh, while I raise one
With difficulty,
Swaying on the front porch,
While pointing at something
In the gray distance.

You see nothing, eh?
Neither do I, Mr. Milkman.

I better hit you once or twice over the head
With this fine old prop,
So you don't go off muttering

I saw *something*.

COLLECTOR'S TWEEZERS

Who let these many bats loose,
All at once,
To flit over the darkening meadow,
Picking someone here, someone there?
The answer is, no one.

Still, think of the terror, the rapture
Of being lifted by a force from on high,
After the glory of the sunset,
Into one of these clouds that loom
Like seaside mansions on the horizon.

It's your old-time religion talking,
You said, my love.
It's just potluck for them and for us.
The answer is still, no one.

THE GREAT PICNIC

Brain lazy as the muddy river over yonder
Where someone's already drowning,
Languidly, the way I feel
In this heat after the burgers,
The hot dogs, the bags of chips
And this warm beer I'm drinking.

Still, you want me to crawl under the blanket
For some dessert.
Wait a little. I'm watching a fat guy
Try to stand on his head, his young wife
Rub sun lotion on her legs.

The one going around with a brown grocery bag
Over his head, do we know him?
He's drawn a funny face on it
With a Magic Marker, and now says
We are to hurry eating sweets,
Or whatever else you intend us to do
Under your new beach blanket.

HOT NIGHT

Longhaired Jesus,
Arms outstretched,
Reeling,
In an open yellow convertible
As he flies down
Santa Monica Boulevard

Magdalene driving with shades on.
Tires screaming.
A dwarf with a monkey
Stepped out of a cab.
White hotels, green taffic lights,
Palm trees swaying darkly.

That and nothing else.
Been here and gone.
The scent of the sea.
The palm trees converging
And parting up ahead.

MY PROGRESS ON STILTS

Old-timer, third-rate Orpheus
Lacking even a make-believe Eurydice,
A thousand million steps
And only now do you notice
These ghostly contraptions attached to your feet.

You're like a windmill on toothpicks.
Don't go near fire.
Don't try to walk on water.
You're teetering, you are about to trip
And fall on your face.

Screech owls and buzzards nest
On your shoulders.
You can see as far as Nebraska.
There's a little house on the prairie
For you to approach and knock.
Three mighty blows with your stilt
And they scatter like popped corn.

The feast of Cerberus is at hand,
You shout.
Latch on, little white hen,
We are going the way of all flesh.

These are the stilts of a melancholy
World drifter talking.

Two straws on their way to the sunset.

We keep the sky company.
Time cannot fall asleep, nor can eternity.
Awake they think
And thinking they deepen the silence.

THE EMPEROR

Wears a pig mask
Over his face.

Sits in a shopping cart,

A red toy trumpet in one hand,
A live fly in the other.

Hey, boogie alley Madonna!

I'm donning my black cape
And my orange wraparound shades

Just for you!

*

The Garden of Eden needs weeding,

And the soda machines don't work.

On the street of Elvis look-alikes
I saw the Klan Wizard in his robes.

I saw the panhandling Jesus
And heard the sweet wind chime in his head.

*

It's horror movie time,
Says the Emperor.

Spiked hair, black flag of bug killers
In his belt,

He helps my frail old mother
Cross the street.

She's charmed and thanks him repeatedly:
"Such a nice boy,"

In the meantime,

Touching the mask's empty eye sockets
With her gloved hand.

*

On the graveyard shift,

Commands the Emperor,

Amplify the roaches crawling up
The kitchen wall.

Let's hear about their tuxes-for-rent places,

Their exotic dancers,

And their witch trials,

If they are the same as the ones we've got.

*

The child in a shoebox smoking
A black cigarillo.

The priest with a fly-catcher
At the altar.

The Emperor and the three-legged dog poet
By his side

Limping down the avenue.

*

Make us see what you see in your head,
We implore.

Okay.

He's climbing a ladder licked by flames.

He wears General Washington's wig and military coat.

He's inside a hamster cage admiring himself in the mirror.

He is playing with a million broken toys.

THE ANNIVERSARY

I'll walk the streets all day today
With my eyes closed.
I won't bring a white cane and a dog.
I won't carry a doomsday sign.
I won't cheat, I won't peek.

Women will march in protest on the avenue
With their breasts bared proudly.
It will feel like New Year's Eve.
Everyone will be wearing a funny hat.
There'll be gorillas in the crowd.
It'll be like Halloween.

I'll brush against thousands of solitudes,
Bowing and muttering my apologies.
There'll be missing children,
One or two murderers and their sweethearts.
Someone with onion on his breath
Will put a cold wristwatch against my ear.
It'll be like silent laughter.

The lines in your hand foretell the future;
The sore feet know the past.
Somewhere hereabouts I sold tropical fish.
I painted the ceilings in a funeral parlor.
I was an usher for a live sex show.

Ten minutes to closing time,
In a matrimonial agency rarely frequented
A bride will wait for me
Dressed in white lace like my grandmother.

At a construction site, fifty stories up,
I will step on a long beam,
And go to the very tip of it,
My arms spread wide to steady myself
With the wind gusting off the river.

There's the Brooklyn Bridge
Like an archer's quiver.
There's the Bowery
Where the dead are never buried.

O unknown bride coming to rescue me,
Walking on that narrow girder in your high-heeled shoes
With your eyes tightly closed,
The seagulls will snatch your veil
Just as your gloved hand reaches for mine.